Benjamin Franklin wanted the wild turkey to be the national bird of the United States.

Turkeys have excellent eyesight during the day.

Look at that!

Turkeys have a strong sense of hearing.

We can hear better than humans.

They can hear insects and other small creatures moving in the grass.

The red, fleshy growth on a turkey's head and neck is called a "snood".

The snood can change in size and color, showing a turkey's mood and health.

Baby turkeys are called "poults".

Mother hens are very protective.

Danger!

If they sense danger, they will make alarm sounds and try to scare away anyone that might harm their poults.

Turkeys are social birds and enjoy being around other turkeys.

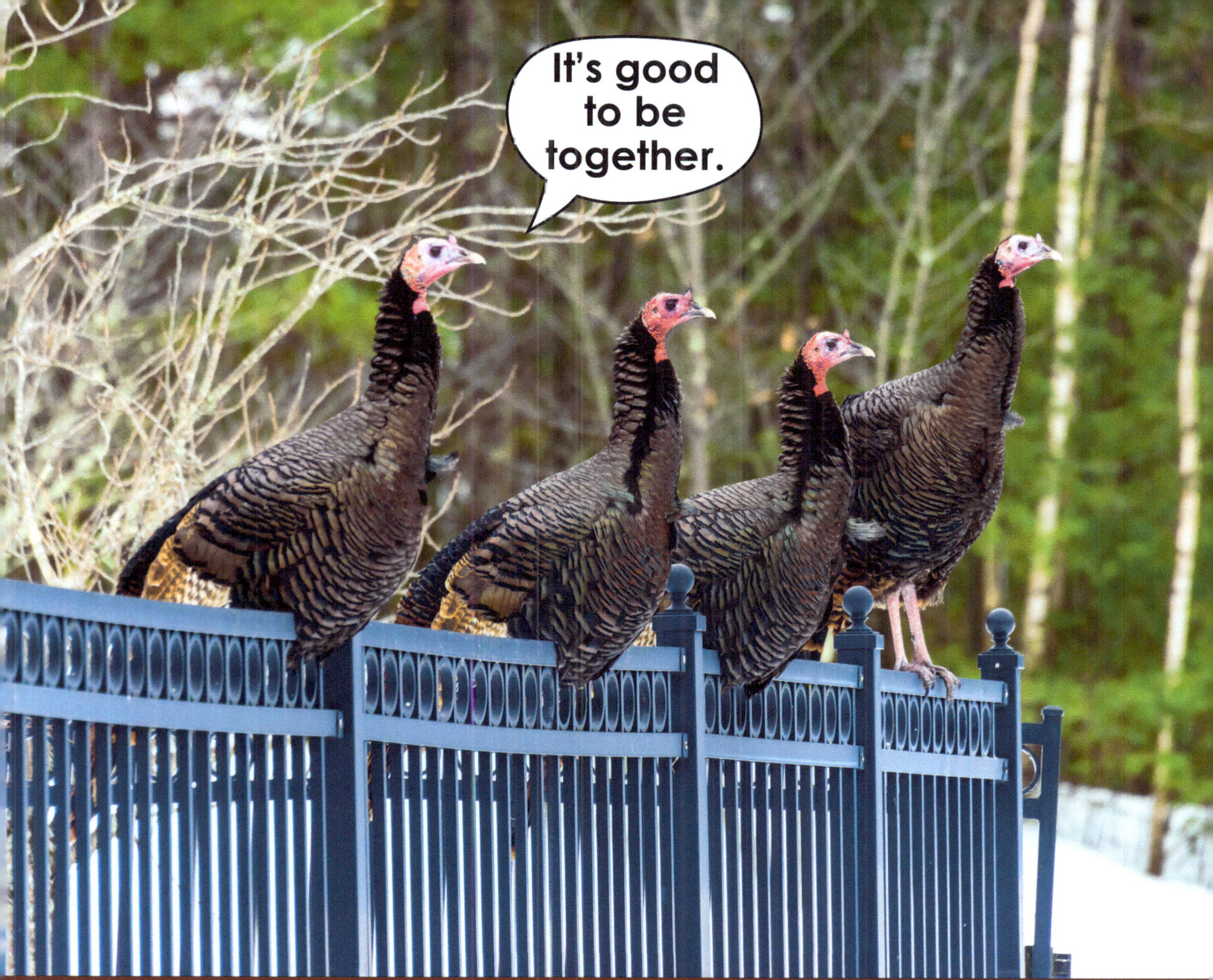

A group of turkeys is called a "flock".

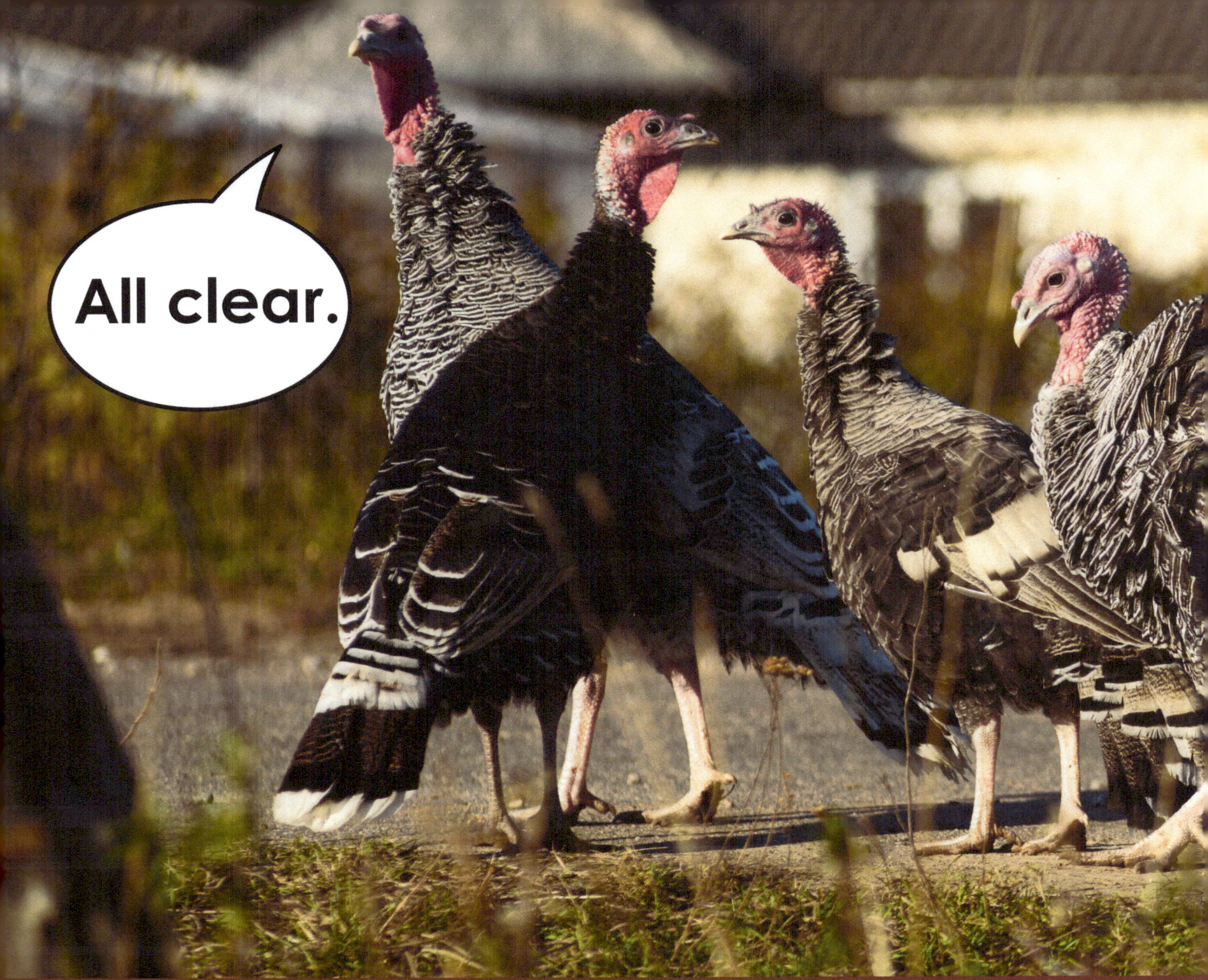

In a flock, turkeys help each other watch for danger.

Turkey flocks are like big families. Moms, dads, and their babies all stick together.

Thanks, sis.

Turkeys are known for making a sound called "gobbling".

The gobble is often used by male turkeys during the breeding season to find a mate.

Hello ladies. *Gobble, gobble.*

Turkeys are "omnivores".

That means they eat both plants and insects.

Turkeys eat a wide variety of plants, like grasses, seeds, berries, fruits and leaves.

Some turkey feathers have special oils that make them waterproof.

Male turkeys are called "toms".

Toms are usually larger and have more colorful feathers than female turkeys.

A tom's tail feathers are called a "fan."

Toms display their fans to attract a mate.

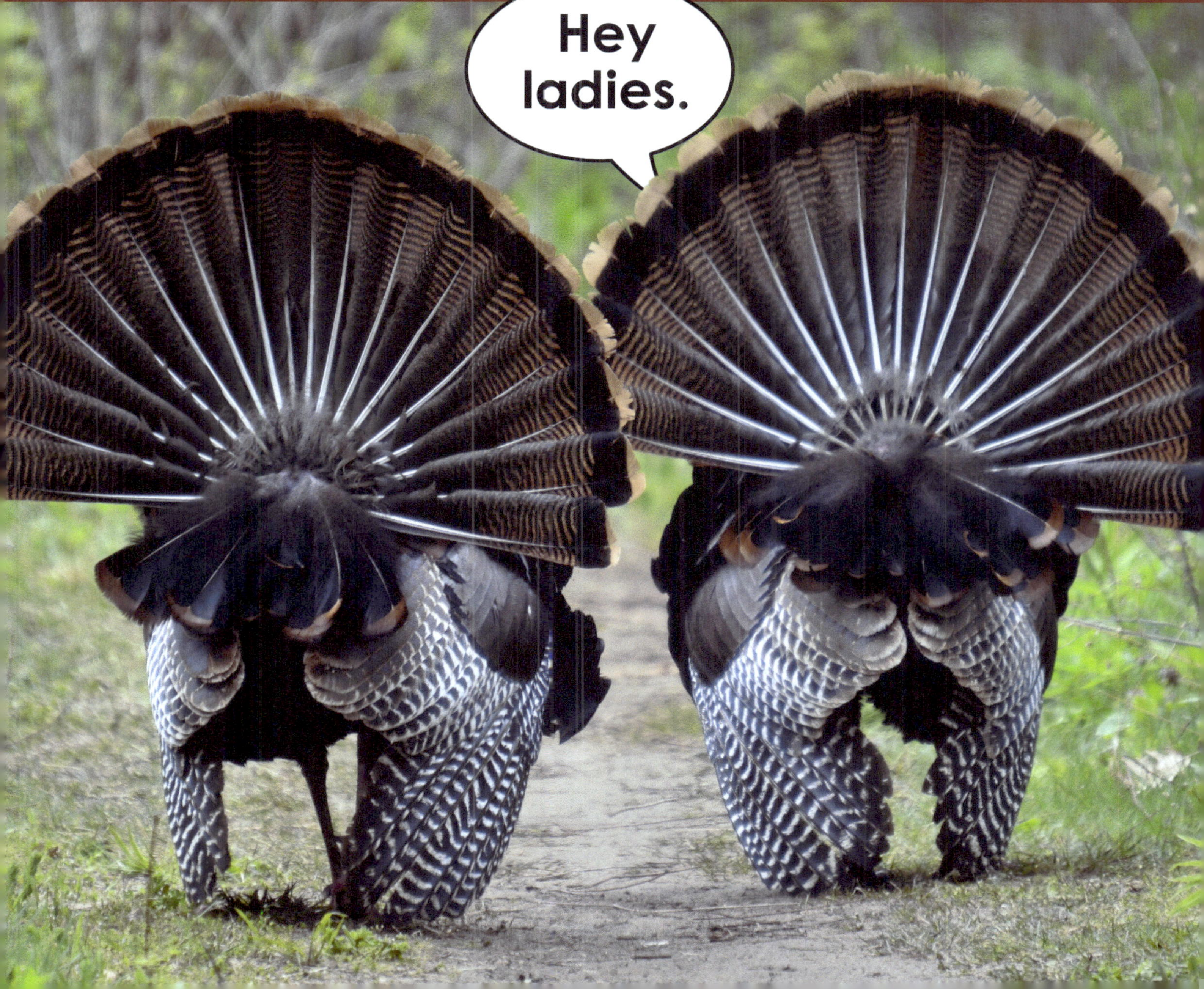

Toms have a "beard", special feathers growing from their chest.

Toms usually have a more colorful head and neck, with red, blue, and white patches of skin.

Look at all these colors.

Hens don't usually gobble, but we do lay eggs.

Hens are smaller than toms and have less colorful feathers.

Some turkey flocks migrate to warmer places when it gets cold.

Turkeys travel together in search of better food and weather.

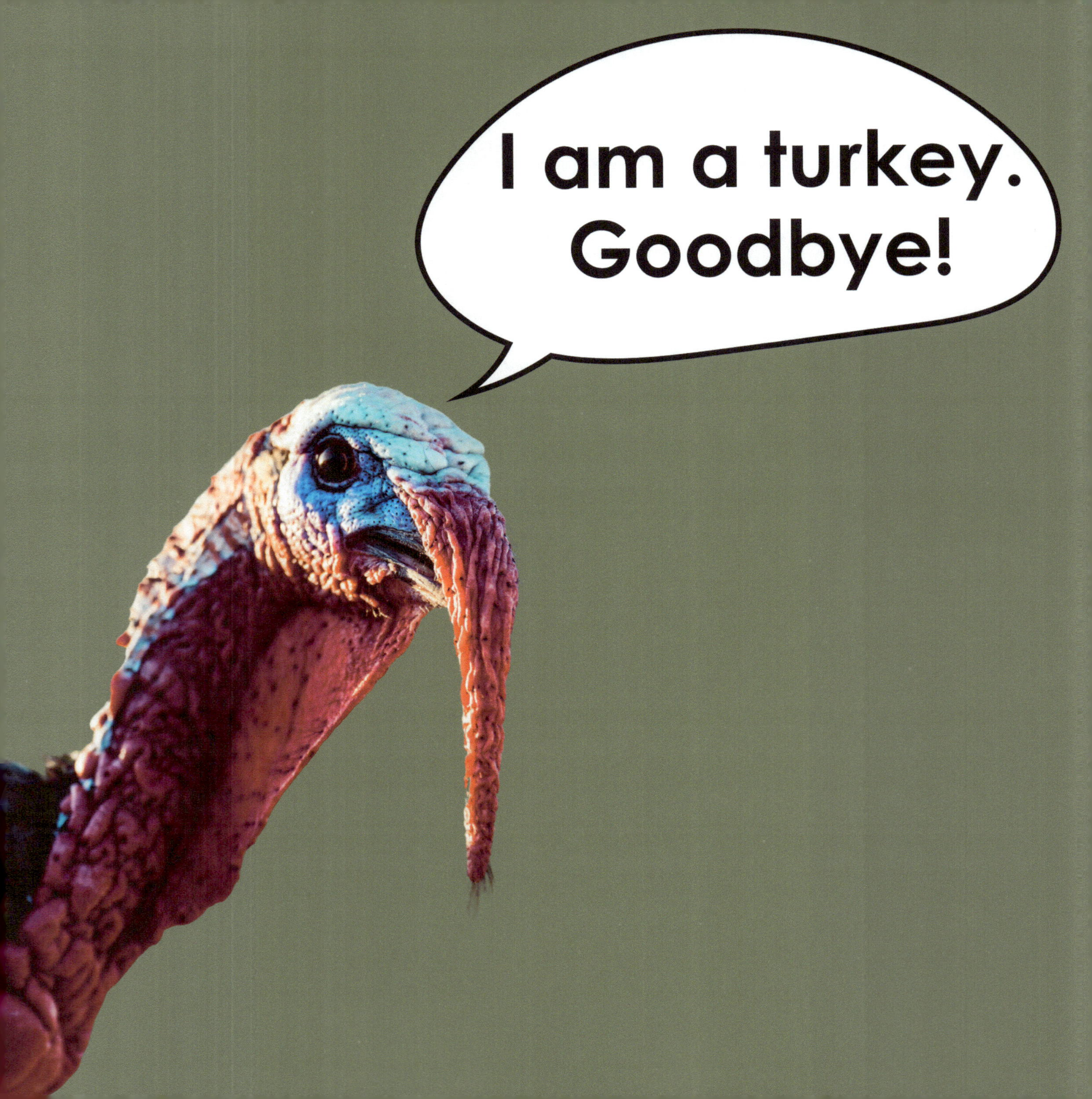
I am a turkey. Goodbye!

Hello parents!

Visit us to find out about new releases and **FREE** offers. We'll let you know when we have a new release coming out and how you can get it for FREE.
And you can cast your vote for what book we make next!

scan here

ActiveBrainsBooks.com

or visit here

---

scan here

or visit here

Let us know what you think. As an independent publisher, your honest reviews mean a lot to us and our business. We'd love to hear from you!

amazon.com/review/create-review/

FOLLOW US on Amazon.

amazon.com/author/activebrainsbooks

ACTIVE BRAINS

ActiveBrainsBooks.com